SAVED

Copyright © 2025 Prudence Brooks
Cover Design: Bethany Pardoe

ISBN: 978-1-968451-01-1

Published by Arcana Poetry Press.
P.O. Box 136 Montgomery, NY 12549
https://www.arcanapoetrypress.com

ARCANA
POETRY PRESS

SAVED

Poems by Prudence Brooks

Dear Reader,

This book contains themes that may be distressing for some readers, including references to child abuse, sexual assault, suicide, self-harm, and disordered eating.

These subjects are approached with care, but I understand they may be difficult to engage with. If you are sensitive to any of these topics, please read gently. Feel free to skip, pause, or put this book down. Take what you need, leave what you must.

This note is not here to censor, but to support your safety as a reader.

I hope reading the poems in this book can offer space for reflection, for release, and if you're ready, for healing — as writing them did for me.

Thank you for being here. Welcome to SAVED.

With deep appreciation,

Prudence

This book is dedicated to every version of myself that
got stepped on, and every part of me
that decided to keep going.

CONTENTS

A fetus suspended in cheap rosé —

I was born already wasted.

STORM WARNING

If you want to tell a profound story, you have to know your audience.

Reader, I know you.

I'm your secret mother, your strange haven. I'm the soft, downy breast your head gravitates toward just before closing your weary eyes. I know what you're here for, and you may be disappointed. You might not discover the calm bunker you're desperate to rest in, you might not dodge the falling power line. You might fry in a giant puddle, shocked with electric agony. I can't stop your death with symbolism. My metaphors won't save you, but they might save me.

You will find an abandoned suicide note more triggering than healing, but you have to understand — this book is not about what you need. This book is my flashlight in the dark staircase, my first step into the fortified basement.

This story is a choice I made to keep surviving.

SUPERNATURAL

If two ghosts have a baby, is she born already invisible?

My mommy and daddy
are the most interesting things about me.
By which I mean, no one ever
says they love me
until they learn how I've been hurt.
I am only charming because I'm different.
I'm only irresistible because I'm see-through.

No one believes I am beautiful without bruises.

If two ghosts have a baby,
and that baby becomes a writer,
does every poem she writes
have to be about the past?
Does she stop existing
the moment she stops looking back?

Which world was I shaped for?
Tell me if I'm dead or living.

Have I always been this transparent?

GIRL

As in – child.

Candy cigarette,

sweet with sin.

Feigning maturity,

I get along

well

with adults.

Submitting

to a man

is what will make me

a good woman.

I'll be grown up

as soon as my hand

grips a stiff shaft.

I'll be loved

if I just open

my mouth.

THE PRETENDING POEM

Let's pretend I had a person for a father

instead of a sticky bar counter,
or a stun gun, or a switchblade.

Let's pretend that when he kissed
my strawberry-scraped knees,
his only intention was to soothe me.

Let's pretend he is not a shaken soda can,
or a bubbling hot dog in the world's microwave
on the cusp of covering us all in entrails.

Let's pretend he did not throw
that plastic picnic table, that TV remote,
that court case.

Let's pretend he didn't pilfer
my sister's Hello Kitty panties
and stash them in a box of his paraphernalia.

Let's pretend she still likes Hello Kitty.

IF NOT WOMAN, CALL ME

from the perspective of my mother

A dead racehorse
beaten aubergine by a tall,
bad-tempered boot.

A missing television remote.
Something meant to guide,
instead lost forever
someplace close to home.

A cup of cold coffee,
Styrofoam feet
coated in a sludge of Stevia —
a bold blend
masking its bitterness.

A twisted, blue dishrag
wrung out in front of company
and hung over the faucet
like it's nothing.

THE EXPLOITATION OF A CHILD
IS THE MOST ACCEPTABLE KIND

My brother and I traverse
to the edge of the woods
where blackberry bushes | ripen

and rot.

The buckets in our hands
are too shallow for the harvest,
much like our narrow throats —
voids for shrunken voices.

When autumn arrives in Indiana,
Bub and I rake titian and amber into piles.
We haul logs from the same clearing
where we split them earlier in the year,
stack them by the wood stove
for convenience.

The only thing an adoptee is good for is labor.
The smartest thing a child can be is useful.

Winter is long and never warm,
even next to the fire. The dog,
gaunt as a ghost,
trembles violently in the snow.
I let him into the house
when our parents aren't home.

I'm afraid he will freeze out there.

I'm afraid that me, my brother,
my beloved mutt —

we will all die here.

INVOCATION

Lord,
set me free.

I heard heaven is
quiet
in the night.
No enraged father hollering.
No coyotes' cries
echoing ominously in the countryside.

I want to wrap
my grandmother's gold crucifix
around my helpless neck
and pull.

I want to huff frankincense
until I   collapse
     at the altar,
gasping —
begging atonement
for my heinous sins.

Every night I say a devotion.

If I shall die before I wake,
I pray the Lord my soul to take.

I like to believe if I strangled myself
with a purple cincture,
if I positioned the prayer candle
to my own mahogany hair,
Saint Peter would cup my molten essence
inside his crystallized hands
to solidify my place inside his palms.

He'd take me home.

RESTRICTION IN THE KEY OF D MAJOR

Eleven years old & gossamer thin —
I pare my waist to the core with a potato peeler
while laboring in Grandmother's
sweltering kitchen. My cotton ears pop
with the sound of spitting grease,
& I distract myself with country songs
on her ancient, wheezing radio.
Kenny Chesney and Martina McBride
become the soundtrack to my demise.
Witnesses
to the suppression of my perverted desires,
my butter-dipped daydreams.   I hold

      my hunger.

I belt out the high note in A Broken Wing
& pretend flying is a natural talent of mine.
A destiny at that.
A girl is worthless
until she weighs less than a feather.

I'm eleven years old & my weak knees
tremble in the ceremonious heat,
but I don't mind because my death procession

is so catchy.
I know static will come, but for now,

I just want to sing.

GO HOME, CHILD

If I had created your death certificate, I
would have written the word *trouble* where
your middle name should go.   I would have preserved
your corpse in cinnamon whiskey and drawn
a crude doodle on your tombstone.

Mom, I hate that you never had a proper funeral.

When they told me you died, the words plopped
off apathetic tongues.   No one lifted a finger for my
grief, so I sawed off both my hands for you. Pressed my
bloody stubs together and said *Our Father*
until my tongue went numb, and my cheeks grew sore,
and the priest blew out the prayer candles,
murmuring,

Go home, child.

As though I knew what it was to be a child.
As though I knew what it was to have a home.

SMALL TALK

I-65 shimmers with morning frost.
It's uncrowded — bare
as Mom's branched tongue.
Her frozen limb whips against the pearl
windows lining her grimace as I brace
for a blizzard.

It's always winter in Mom's mouth.

She asks me about school — I say it's fine.
I ask her about work — she says it's fine.

We waste our time together.

She jabbers about the upcoming softball season,
gossips about my swim coach
with the weird posture.
Mom says she only stands that way
to make her tits look perkier.
She's probably right,
but I'm not sure why it matters.

I tell her I saw Mary Anne
buying a pink pregnancy test at the CVS.
The only way to bond with Mom
is to talk down on someone with her.

Last night,
I carved my father's name
onto the inside of my thigh with a pen knife.
Smeared the blood across my finger,
deliberately licked it off before I went back in.
This morning, I told my mom,

Yeah, I slept great.

Thanks for asking.

ANOR-HEX-IA

I discovered witchcraft
while s p r a w l e d
on my Grandmother's coarse ginger carpet,
reading diet tips in People Magazine.

I learned <u>a body is a curse</u>.
A person is a vessel for a **void** to pose in.

So, I surrounded myself with feathery girls
and brash boys bound in thorns.
I snapped | my frail spine into twigs,
cast a circle of sanctuary around me.
Famine kept me functional.
Hunger kept me safe.

My vivacious grin was a spell
that protected me from questions,
but inside,
the black dahlia had taken root.
As years passed, blood turned to tar.
My upper lip grew Twiggy limbs,
thin wisps of peach trees.

Arms forged of cast iron —
I couldn't lift my hands above my head.
I was dying, but it didn't faze me.
I'd burn myself at the stake
before buying bigger jeans.
I'd pour gasoline down my gaping thorax,
touch the torch to my wheezing heart

if it meant I could be smaller.

PORTRAIT OF AN UNGRATEFUL ADOPTEE

I've been caught biting the hand
that feeds me.

I go further and tear the whole thing off —
it's always been a dead limb anyway.

Before I was an empty frame on the mantel, I
was a golden poker stoking the fireplace. I tried
to warm a home with missing insulation and gaps
in the windows. I wore burns like Girl
Scout badges, every scar proof I would
singe my palms to carry my family's sins.
Each crimson patch, a promise I whispered
to my sister in the night —

I won't let them hurt you.

The last time I martyred myself for monsters
I was bent over the lazy chair, black belt
scorching my flesh.   I stared at the dark green
carpet and bit my lip, seeking a pain
I had reign over.   I can taste the copper even now.
It reminds me of hunger.

I have a spite inside me that beats like a heart,
that speaks like a bear's mouth.   I write poems
that reek of bile, so you know they come
from my gut.   I have cruelty writhing in my womb,
wet as blood and wailing for milk.
As it is birthed, I unbutton my shirt.

It feasts.

FOOD LOG

- A quarter cup of pulp-free orange juice
  to get my metabolism moving.
- Gossip in the cafeteria with a couple saltines.
- A Diet Coke I could only afford
  by scouring the bleachers for dropped dimes.
- For supper, one hard-boiled egg
  and three excruciating hours of exercise.

I've been feeling giddy and sick
after a third stick of spearmint gum
and a cup of crushed ice.

My brother and I sit at the scratched yew table,
peeling the skin from our supper,
humming The Foundations in harmony.
We tap our feet in sync on the stained linoleum.
I sprinkle a bit of pepper,
he adds a dash of salt.
We talk sets, reps, numbers.

When you're born in a barren pantry,
you learn to love through scarcity.
We communicate through the rumbles
in our tummies. We feel most like family
when we're hungry.

We only seem to connect
through the broken parts.

ROACH

Did you know the average cockroach
can survive for a month without food?

My record of resilience is a week,
but I'm not only a single roach.
My fractured form is a colony
squeezing itself beneath baseboards,
shimmying behind dusty picture frames.

I'm a horde of household pests
contaminating every surface I touch.
My resentments swiftly reproduce
in dark, oval casings under the fridge,
maliciously morphing every few months.
I'm an adult in my childhood.
A child in my adulthood.

Even the doctor calls me cyclical.
Even my mother named me nuisance.

American cockroaches
can lay up to 90 eggs in their lifetime,
and that's how I persevere
in hostile environments.
By being my own swollen mother.
My own bright-eyed child.

My own indestructible species.

WHEN ASKED FOR MY FAMILY'S
MEDICAL HISTORY

I tell them I'm not sure where it started,
but I'm certain of how it will end.

Father has bleached bones —
ancient and encircled
by buzzing flies —
he will never really die.
Father will be fossilized.

Brother is a clone of brother
who is a clone of mother
who is a clone of Eve
in her sparse loincloth.

Curiosity is death among kin.

Little sister is a tweak of strings,
a chirpy melody developing.
Bigger sister is a pallid corpse.
There's no authentic metaphor
for absence.
Middle sister is a pair of soiled socks
crumpled in the corner —
worn out and stepped on.
Threadbare and longing
to lay against warm skin.

Is there anything more to know?

Yes.

But there's nothing more I can tell you.

BUZZED

Chunks of basil-faded hair litter the grimy kitchen tile. Liz crops my locks close to my scalp, selecting the first setting on her roommate's clippers. I ask her to shear until I say stop, so she makes an egg of me. I'm hatching again — bursting from my casing — wingless and translucent. Slippery with El Jimador and sticky with lime juice.

Beyonce's Lemonade plays from Liz's phone speaker. *Okay ladies, now, let's get in formation.* I don't relate, but I subconsciously bob my foot in rhythm. I was a fidgety child, fraternizing during quiet time and straying from the queue too often. I stand out in the worst ways. Liz sings along like she, too, is rich in gems, like she's ridden low in the El Camino with the Carters. I don't know where she gets the confidence.

It's important that an impulsive girl
like me has insecurities.

The most efficient muzzle for a mouthy broad
is doubt.   Shame keeps me leashed to reality.
I'm shaving my head because I'm restless —
persistently uneasy and unkempt.   My baldness is
a silent way of barking at the back door,
a muted plea for freedom.   I don't even need
to feel good.   I just lust for something different.
I'm strongest in the shadows, so I take the shape
of infestation.   Preserving wholeness is naïve.   I
minced myself into a litter of insects
when I was five and my father said
No one is coming to save you.

I needed to know some version of me
might make it out.

I DO IT FOR THE VINE

Point the camera at me

as long as it only catches glimpses.

I can be clever for six seconds.

I am gorgeous in small doses.

It's the moment right after the red light

shuts off

that my stomach is wrung like the slender neck

of a wounded bird.

The moment when no one is watching anymore,

but I'm still performing.

Staging joy because, in my heart, I hate myself

and I hate my life

and I'm trying to film something different

into existence. I'm gathering an army of avatars,

building a bunker in the comment section.

I hate to be alone.

PANIC ATTACK AT THE GROCERY STORE

I linger in the pasta aisle staring at a package of Annie's shells. They look incredible, orange cheese screaming at me from a wrinkled cardboard box. I study the calories & fat content, scanning through a list of malignant preservatives. I'm horrible at math. I try to calculate how much comfort I deserve, but my multiplication tables stow sugar packets underneath their wobbly feet. When I place the box of Annie's into my basket, my knees buckle like a rickety bridge.

I can't hold the weight of wanting.

QUEEN OF THE GET THROUGH

is Daddy's little princess, all grown up. Each gleaming jewel glued to her tiara is an unhealed bruise; every ring encircling her finger is another arrest. She wears her checkered past like a party dress, pretends she didn't steal her outfit from the picnic table at Tuhey Park. Wherever she goes, she takes her hometown with her, and it shrouds her in spikes, tints her teeth red and rusty.

Queen of the Get Through needs mood stabilizers, but thinks medication is a middle-class thing. She's sour about her upbringing, and resentful of yours, too. Queen of the Get Through is defensive. She forged emotional armor in a flaming crib; she knows staying alive requires a shield.

Queen of the Get Through knows the only way to get through is to get on with it. Stand up. Clean the kitchen. Go to work. Only the privileged think it's a special feat to keep enduring.

The rest of us just call it Monday.

THE BIPOLAR SPEAKS

I love this time of year.

You can pretend your swollen eyes
are from allergies, and we can reminisce
on all of our gruesome suicide attempts.
The blare of a man's angry car horn
as you step in front of his Honda.
The steel mattress made of train tracks.
The box cutter with the red blade.
The hollow pill bottle next to the bed.

I love this time of year.

Have you started smoking again yet?
You can brush your teeth all you want —
every one of them will still fall out.
You should have learned from your Daddy
that nothing we do really matters.

I love this time of year.

You can water a plant, and it will still die
simply because you forgot to re-pot it,
or the wind blew in the wrong direction.

I love this time of year.

I DON'T WANT TO GET BETTER

I want to get much worse.

Collapse on scabbed knees
in the heart of a murky bog
and say *Thank you*
as I sink.

Larynx cloaked in spongy peat,
damp tongue tickled by dragonflies —
I want to give myself to grief

totally.

I will do more than marry my madness —
I'll offer my life for her.
I'll stand on the side closest to the street
while I hold her hand and sacrifice myself
when white coat colonizers come busting
through the door, demanding compliance.

They could wedge a pry bar
into my clamped jaw,
stuff my throat with chalk, etch

insubordinate

into my records until I'm little more
than a dazed lab rat, nothing
but a red buzzer.
Lithium won't save anything.

That's just a different kind of death.

IT'S QUITTIN' TIME

So I slacken my wind-up spine with a drink, or two drinks, or a pint of cheap rum. I mix Sailor Jerry's with citrus, squeezing the juice from a shriveled lemon that's been slowly dying in my kitchen. Precariously carrying my drink to the bedroom, I spill a few droplets on the freshly polished floor and instinctively wipe them up with my sweat-drenched sock. Upstairs, my body collapses on a jaundiced mattress and I ache with Conor Oberst through the cheap headphones I stole from Dari Mart. I never listen to him out loud because my roommate hates sad music.

She hates sad people, too.

Young and immune to hangovers — every night I drown myself in a hot spring brimming with hooch until I wake bundled in a fluffy green towel. When the apricot dawn begs me to take a bite, I dutifully open my mouth. I nibble on her crisp ascent and schlep across town to sell my wellness. Abandon my autonomy. Die a little death, like every poor person I know.

I finish my shift stinking like fried feces and everyone avoids me on the bus. Whatever. My stop is across from the liquor store on Lawrence and 11th. The lights are too bright, but the cashiers call me pretty and share their cigarettes.

Breaching the threshold to my address is different. It's a hesitant step into cold water. We got a new roof recently, but I still feel exposed here. The coziest thing I know is the warm trickle of liquor slinking down my throat, sneakily eroding my sensibilities.

Does every home have to be solid?

I'M NOT PRETTY WHEN I'M NAKED

Nudge your nose to mine.
Note the furrow
where black crows gather —
their ridged feet unfurled
across chiffon skin.

Notice the shallow ruts
where my adult acne
peeled rubber —
rogue hairs throwing parties
when the tweezers leave town.
I'm not pretty unpixellated.
I'm undesirable up close.

Snarling viciously when cornered,
I glimpse my father in every shadow.
I have always known
I will die in the dark.

He was the first person to teach me I am brutal;
who showed me I can spit.
I'm not beautiful inside or out, but
I'm a terrific shot with a wood grip revolver.

There's nothing honey here
but the trick of light
pirouetting across amphitheater eyes
in yellow slippers, tied too tight.
I'm alluring to everyone
in different hues —
at certain angles —
but when the golden hour ends
and the coal lamp goes out,

I'm just another disappointment.

BLOOD MONEY

My psychiatrist tells me to relax, but rent is due in three days, and I have my weekly session at the plasma center tonight. I'm weak-kneed, scatterbrained, and I think I might be dying, but I don't tell anyone. They're all dying, too. None of us acknowledge the costumed elephant taking a shit in the middle of the room. We simply spritz Febreze and earn rewards for attending the circus. I've racked up so many points at the plasma center they greet me by name. It's the only place I'm famous. After my veins are wasted and the needle extracted, my head spins like a malnourished model at the helm of the catwalk. I, too, have ceded my body to capitalists. I am also hungry. Cupping my head with sacrificial hands, I stagger to the ATM behind the seedy Carl's Jr. and cash the donation card so I can buy something to eat.

It keeps on like this. Swallowing my body and calling it thrifty. The case worker names it necessary. Like someone must be starving for anyone else to be satisfied. My psychiatrist treats me like a child — *I'm rubber, and you're glue.* Every fearful tear that slips from my green, desperate eyes bounces off his armor of entitlement. He tells me *Joy is free* while vengeful ants leave scarlet footprints indented in my skin. He claims I shouldn't worry; it's just a stress rash. He's unconcerned by what's bothering me. When I tell him pleasure costs as much as anything and I can't afford to be happy, he writes **defiant** in his notes and sends me home

hopeless.

TWENTY-TWO

found me
homeless/porous —
absorbing every vague scent,
every scuttle of rock around me.
I lumbered through the streets,
heaving a shabby suitcase behind me,
bumming drags from wet cigarettes.

I listened to far-fetched stories
dribbling down stubbled chins
and told my own tall tales,
only as true as they needed to be.

I snagged the waist
of an undercover chameleon
who would later cross the street
when she saw me coming.

Secrets always find the light.

I drew a heart around a boy
and wished him into existence.
Taught him to love me.
Screamed at him, pleading,
SHOW ME HOW TO COMPARE TO HER.

I slept in a twin bed with a friend
I loved but never kissed,
lost her in a manner worse than any death.

Learned there are many things
dead and breathing.

Learned that sometimes
you shouldn't even check the pulse.
Just point your eyes ahead

and keep moving.

WHAT YOU'RE ABOUT TO READ
IS A NIGHTMARE

I dream of eating the rotten persimmons

smushed in the grass behind Grandma's house.

I wonder if they'll make my stomach ache.

It seems something is always hurting.

If not me, then the rabbit twitching

in the left lane.

I don't know how anyone heals a broken bone

while others are under rubble;

it seems everyone around me is callous.

They wish I could take a shot of whiskey

without a swig of Diet Coke,

but I've never been that carefree.

Never been that cool.

I dream of fingers smudged

with purplish pulp —

of eating persimmons in October

until my stomach twists and trips,

spilling black sludge and bile

across frosted grass.

Can you call it a nightmare

if you never wake up?

Can you call it living if you sleep in a noose?

Mommy, come here. | My stomach hurts.

SLEEPOVER WITH MY BIPOLAR

Midnight / / Stars strung across dark blue sky
like lustrous pearls over a dead girl's neck —
every day feels like suiting up for a funeral.
Tonight feels like composing my own elegy.

Two AM / / The room stinks of peeling rubber.
Thoughts speed by; my heartbeat accelerates.
I'm a sleek race car with nicked brakes,
hurtling into the grass trap.

Four AM / / Drinking.
Absorbing liquor like a cliff consumes a wave,
because what is there but cheap whiskey?
Who am I if not my father?
I don't care about "potential" anymore.

Six AM / / The world will wake soon.
The clock's corpse resuscitated,
the queue of contestants lining up.
The competition doesn't stop because I'm tired.

Eight AM / / I'm alive and I'm not sure
how that's possible. Humming Rilo Kiley,
I force my freckled, crooked knees into jeans
and pour a bowl of Cheerios. No milk.
It's bittersweet, isn't it? The way morning

keeps coming.

THIS LONELINESS IS GETTING
HARD TO ROMANTICIZE

Strings of mucus slip
even when I sniff in quickly,
trying to slurp the ooze back
into my nostril.
Without a doubt,
ACHOO / / more, more
green goo comes flying from me.
Infected. Infectious.
Everyone knows I'm sick,
and they love it.
Isn't it impressive?
How I turn filth into a fashion statement?

The loneliness is a cold I can't shake;
it's more exhausting every minute.
I think I'm contracting pneumonia.
My breath — shallow as a kiddie pool.
My lungs — filling with fluid.

This is how I drown myself.

POEM IN PLACE OF A SEDATIVE

It begins at the Big Bang,
my father's fisted meteor
colliding with the bathroom mirror.
Blood spattering from his knuckles
against toothpaste-dappled glass.
Mom crying out,
reaching for a phone with a cut cord.

It's this early memory, these crimson specks
seeping into my brain that explain
the lack of evolution in my confidence.
My reflection tainted with violence —

I can't seem to stand up straight.

I look at my hands
and see scars of my ancestors,
white moonflowers drenched in starlight.
This desert between my ears has been
colonized a million times,
but not a single flag can get a grip
on my cracked soil.

I am resistant to "civilization."

The doctor says this new pill will bring rain,
will sow seeds and evolve organisms.
I pick up the bottle from the pharmacy
knowing I will forget to take them.

Knowing part of it is not forgetting at all.

DRAFTING A SUICIDE NOTE

There are parts of my body I have never seen and there is much of me I will never know.

This next part is both a choice and a prophecy, a coming and a going. Anyone reading this letter is looking for answers. I don't have them. Everyone wants to hold someone responsible. I plead guilty.

The truth is, I'm just tired. Tired of weeping at women stabbed on the subway, weary of dodging covert cameras in the workplace. Sick of joints that pop like soda tabs and teeth that ache from slick, candied fibs. We're all dwindling erasers, rubbing our round heels on the ground, hoping that yesterday will disappear. We're all writers, ripping pages out of notebooks, trying to dream up a different plot.

The thing is, I'm out of papers. I'm a limp, creased spine. Dry of marrow. Devoid of potential. Believe me when I say, it has been over for me for a while now.

I know anyone reading this is in disbelief and I take some pleasure in your shock. I watched your eyes roll back inside their sockets like glass marbles the night I bawled on the front stoop, frenetically rocking back and forth, breathlessly moaning,

I want to die. I want to die.

You checked your phone while I sobbed, and I learned there is no other way to be heard.

I told you I could commit to something.

E-GIRL CRIES FOR HELP

I want to KMS!   jk jk.

But for real,

I gtg.

I literally
CANNOT

anymore.

I found a porn on VHS
in my hoggish father's sock drawer
next to a book about eating pussy.

I guess he shouldn't have demanded
I do his chores.

What a long, strange trip

it's been,

but I don't wish I was never here.

I'm just past my expiration —

or cooked

  as the kids say.

If another dead infant comes across my screen,

I'll unalive myself

by daybreak.

I don't think it was a joke, after all.

PAIN AS

a bitchy, brunette bartender. Pain as a spiked drink. Pain as a mean mug. Pain as a wildfire. Pain as a controlled burn. Pain as a croak in the throat. Pain as an echo in the sewer. Pain as the barn I grew up in. Pain as the field where I'll be buried. Pain as an altar, pain as a shrine. Pain as a shepherd. Pain as a commandment. Pain as a mistake. Pain as bloody sheets. Pain as something that stains. Pain as a thing I have never not known.

Pain as circling vultures. Pain as a pet corn snake. Pain as a pesticide. Pain as a boot to the scampering roach. Pain as not a metaphor. Pain as much too real. Pain as an endless equation. Pain as a school bell on the brink of ringing. Pain as an overworked child. Pain as a flushed face. Pain as a hissy fit. Pain as predator. Pain as prey. Pain as a blind fold. Pain as an evil you will never understand. Pain as a tattered map. Pain as an outdated manual. Pain as the star I follow.

Pain as the God I've lost.

HOW TO DIE BEAUTIFULLY
(and other lessons learned from nature)

Clutch a thermos of cold green tea

under a blushing sun; overdose on chlorophyll.

Frolic through the savannah in lace panties;

feed on the ephemeral light, the temporary

high of starving. By autumn, your carotenes

will have kittens, a body jaundiced.

A woman losing limbs —

dropping dry, wispy hairs.

The hickory trees blown bare;

you are the cause of your abscission.

No one cares that you are dying.

They only care if you are beautiful.

THERE IS SOMETHING WRONG WITH MY BRAIN (IN THE SEXIEST WAY POSSIBLE)

A skunk scampers across the sod of my synapse.
It burrows its snout and bends over,
spraying until my mind stinks of disillusion.

When I say there is something wrong
with my brain, what I mean is that
from the moment I entered this world,
I've been looking for a way out.

I've been searching for a door marked EXIT

but all I find are two-way mirrors.

I am captive in this barren abyss,
this dry and colorless chasm
that delivers nothing but misgivings.
My cranium fogs up as though I've blown
on a cold window, but I swear,
I'm just trying to get close enough to reach you.

All the lesbian metalsmiths
and the finance degree DJs
slip their hands beneath my sweaters,
trail their fingers across my rounded cheeks.
They tell me I look like Maisie Williams,
that I feel so much like a fantasy.
I try not to think of this
when they are making love to me.
Try not to think of them watching someone else
lounge naked inside my eyes.
At the end of the day,
I can be touched and touched and touched

and still ache.

SOMETHING VAGUE

My microphone is soaking wet and static.

I'm standing at the lip of a blustery cliff
getting drenched by a wicked Pacific storm.

No wait,
I'm shackled in a fluorescent hospital bed.

Actually,
my crossed fingers are clutching the corners
of a slot machine at the casino
past the outlet mall.

Nowhere is anywhere and my reality
is only a combination of fantasies
too specific to be entirely fiction.
Too outlandish to be complete fact.
The truth is,

I know as much as you do.

IF I DON'T WRITE THIS POEM, I'LL DIE

I've been melancholic my whole life.

Decades revolving around the Earth's

ramshackle axis, fingers curled tightly

around a scratching ballpoint pen.

Why are the bed sheets not bound

into a baby blue noose?

Why am I not aerating antifreeze

in a long-stemmed wine glass?

Don't make me say it in stanzas.

I'm a coward & I know it. Champion

of dubiety — I love pretending there's

something to ponder. As though existence

isn't just chemicals, & there's meaning to

our laughter, to our thick, hot tears.

I slam a shot of Tito's to equalize

the aftertaste of a stale Eucharist.

I'm desperate for a reason to stay here.

SIDE EFFECTS

The side effect of taking Klonopin is developing a fine tremor. The side effect of a fine tremor is struggling to open up the childproof packaging your prescription is delivered in. The side effect of struggling to open up is struggling to shut down. The side effect of struggling to shut down is swallowing more Klonopin. The side effect of swallowing more Klonopin is dizziness. The side effect of dizziness is a spinning sprinkler in the brain. The side effect of getting drenched is shivering. The side effect of shivering is a laptop playing a Roman Catholic mass on YouTube while you swig directly from an open bottle of King's Estate. You repeat the priest's prompts to an illuminated screen. *Peace be with you.* The congregation chants back, *And with your spirit.* The side effect of responding is wondering if you mean it.

The side effect of doubt is panic. The side effect of panic is sitting down in the shower, feeling the warm water wash over your brittle spine, wishing your boiler was large enough to fill a bathtub. The side effect of wishing is forgetting that what you once wished for is everything you have now. Anxiety is a different beast when spiked with benzos, and the side effect of a drugged enemy is time to react. The side effect of having time is wanting more of it. The side effect of wanting is wanting

is wanting   is wanting

DISSECTING THE THEME

It's a metaphor for attachment.

The dividends of my desperate form, the insistence that I am but an aggregate of disorganized fragments is an indicator of lingering faith. A parish is not a family reunion, but a professional sport. We call the congregation our community, but there's underlying competition. I miss this half-baked fib, dipped in powdered sugar. I still fiend for the sweet blood of the sacrament. I pray the breached vein is a channel to the heart and sink my mandible in deeper. Did you know cockroaches sever their wings when they choose a permanent mate? This is why they were given sanctuary on Noah's wooden ark. Like me, they have a sick sense of devotion.

It's a metaphor for grief.

Cockroaches also mourn their dead. I like to think they hold a vigil, that they recite a Prayer for the Faithful Departed, but their aisle to the altar has been decimated by bitter elements. There is nothing alive in this climate that isn't suffering. There's no one that isn't confused.

It's a metaphor for self-preservation.

This explanation is a way of saying I crave community and solitude. I desire ritual and liberty. How do I persevere without fracturing entirely? Is there a freedom that doesn't leave me forsaken?

I need a place to gather.
I need a place to gather myself.

ONCE

I slept in a bolted cellar,

woke in an unzipped tent.

Buried a three-legged kitten

beneath the soil and leaves

scattered around the tapped maple tree.

Hardly felt a sting in my eye.

That's when I knew I was dead —

or grown –

one of the two.

Trekked in secondhand stilettos

over freshly turned dirt,

told an eager-fingered grief

I only dress up for funerals.

Dressed down for him,

ebony skirt hiked up to my waist,

frayed tights around my ankles.

Fell hard from the monkey bars

under a full moon and howled

like only a white wolf

howls. A wild thing,

I am.

I shed. I whimper.

I bite.

MY DEPRESSION IS A WEAPON

The psychic chainsaw has gone awry.

I only intended to hack down
my own bark brushed heart.
I didn't mean to cleave you open.

Or maybe, subliminally, I did.

The serrated knife thrusts
into your chubby gut,
and you're silent.
Just like you're always
silent.
You avert your eyes,
but appear unsurprised
when I twist the blade.
I'm not as tender as I once imagined.
I'm not soft when I am frightened.

My fist —
the DJs jaw at midnight,
tightly clenched and pulsing.
I raise my voice like a tattered flag.
This is a war over nothing.
This is *misery loves company*.
I can say I didn't mean it —

but that doesn't mean it didn't hurt.

TIMELINE (nonlinear)

fuchsia streak pickled in chlorine, bound in elastic // Em and I kissing in the pool, hoping her mom doesn't come home early // an altar in the forest, a procession of salmon slipping over stones // notes on a piano as I amble down the aisle // a book hurled at my head, a lamp shattered behind me // candy apple hair and black nail polish // she looks like she would be all boot, but really, she's the softest pink slipper // him calling me by another's name // me crying and letting him finish anyway // learning that consent is relative // that horror is inevitable // committing myself to something // anything // before it's too late.

I DON'T WANT TO HEAL MY INNER CHILD, I WANT TO GIVE HER A BARBED WIRE BASEBALL BAT

Of course the queer girl plays softball. First kiss quite literally in the closet, baby girl spills scarlet across the bathroom tile the night her adoptive father throws a Bible at her. I want to tell her not to take that box cutter to her own skin. I want to tell her to sneak to his bedroom instead, to show his exposed throat what **real sin** looks like. I don't want to heal my inner child, I want to nurture her rage. Mama said dust is beautiful, so be nothing at all. Be only an annoyance a man can wipe away with his pointer finger. A trembling voice the priest can hardly hear amongst the congregation. Daddy may have run me over but it was my mother who demanded I lay down in front of the pickup truck.

My inner child and I stroll away from all of our childhood homes at once, drizzling a trail of gasoline behind us. We spark up an American Spirit and send the itching match. Close our eyes and grin up at the smokey sky. The screams sound like lullabies | to us.

DIVIDE / DETACH

If I speak of anorexia

as something other than myself.

If I call her Ana,

affix a freckled face and dirty blonde hair.

If I rise like a floured messiah,

splitting open at the top,

like I was born again in a bakery.

If I break us apart like communion bread,

can I still say I have faith in something?

BIPOLAR IS BORED AND RENAMES HERSELF

Bipolar pulls the blanket over her eyes.
She's trying to be a good girl and **go to sleep**
like Doc demanded. But Bipolar's bruised knees
are knotted like seaweed in the sheets,
intrusive thoughts prickling like stonefish
at her feet.

Bipolar decides she wants to be a shy redhead.
No, a blue-haired manic dream.
No, a brunette housewife | wiping
her brow beside an oppressive stove.
Bipolar seems to think that if she
looks different, she'll feel different,
but that's never been the case.

Bipolar is restless
and looking for a new way to say:

I am a reinforced safe with a glitchy combination;
you will never fully crack me open.

I have been moving through moods like seasons,
and I've still not destroyed all of my crops.

I am a tornado chaser; I know these winding roads.
I can read these blustery skies like the Bible passages
I memorized in the second grade.

I need you to trust me.

THE EDITOR

glares disapprovingly from her gilded Bergere
chair, jabbing its pointed feet into the folds
of my cranium. She paves a red ink road
over the untouched foxglove
and rips violas up like weeds,
claiming that the truth is unsightly.
Unprofitable, too.

My therapist tells me to imagine the editor
as an object and the first thing that comes
to mind is a silver colander.
It is filled to the brim with secrets
that refuse to fit through the holes
caked in blood. Maybe it's marinara sauce.
I pray it's Prego — something soluble.

All I can do is run water over it religiously.
Maybe if I disintegrate the blood,
if I break the secrets down into smaller pieces,
they will slip through the openings with more
ease.

Praying that one day my words will run free
across the page with no line breaks
or tabs shifting
or worry about who's watching.

I'm not trying to hate the editor,
because hating the editor is hating myself.
There's nothing creative about self-loathing.
The editor is not a colander,
or a red pen, or an asphalt roller.

The editor is me —
ten years old, being hit hard by my dad
in front of my friends and trying not to cry
because **I don't want to look like a baby.**

The editor is me —
three years old, rigid
with shock as my mother shrieks at me
from a hospital bed
and the nurse drags me away
by a malnourished wrist.

The editor is me —
18, pinned down in a cornfield
and taught the consequences
of existing as a girl alone
in a den of lions,
only the lions are men,
and the men are always the same.

But the editor can change.
The editor can still do anything.

We have all the time in the world
to get this right.

DREAM STUDY

If you dream of a yellow slide, it's a sign of a new era. If there's a snarling tiger at the bottom of the chute, it means you're terrified of what comes next. If the tiger is pink, you are a boy. If the tiger is blue, you are a girl. A dream is the only safe place to color outside the lines. If you dream of your mother washing dishes, you miss her. If she brandishes a knife, she misses you. If she cleaves your chest in half and you don't wiggle, it means you never stopped grieving. If she places your heart inside the freezer, it means neither did she. If you dream that you are dreaming, you are lucid. If you are lucid, this is your chance to fly. If you know you can fly, why don't you?

You're in control.

ALTAR GIRL THROWS THE PRAYER CANDLE AND SETS THE WHOLE PARISH ON FIRE

I wake up every Sunday in a pleated, plaid skirt.

Scratchy white socks creep

toward gnarled knees,

sneaking beneath my polycotton hem

like the fat-bellied cat under the taproot

of a red oak tree. Soon,

there will be six wet kittens.

There will be manicured fingers

where the fabric sits against my skin,

clumps of soil where the empty plains

across my chest sprawl out.

I will memorize the lyrics to Teenagers by MCR

and learn how to write erotic poetry.

I don't know it yet,

but the world is more than a church,

and the church is bigger than God.

I don't have to keep carrying things for men

who demand I walk on my knees.

I don't have to keep making excuses for women

who smack their daughters' doubtful mouths.

I don't have to do anything.

~~CATHOLIC~~

A church is a vase
where greedy stems wash their feet
while dropping petals drown.

An aisle is a swift red river.
An altar is a wrathful ocean.
Sticky fingered, innocent children
are swept to a rogue sea.

No one cares if an orphan girl hates herself,
because grief keeps a mutt on her tether.

A parish is the oldest kind of prison,
and religion stunts your growth
as you push against the ceramic walls
of an impossibly small planter.
No one escapes without completely
uprooting themselves.
No one heals without redefining sacrifice.

But they do escape.
                         They do heal.

You're allowed to believe in anything.

WHEN YOU'RE AN ANOREXIC POET
EVERY BITE IS A METAPHOR

I watch it kicking its flippers rhythmically through the alfredo sauce and spinach tortellini. It is a tennis ball cloaked in goosebumps, served between strings of my lover's lost hairs. It is the rounded tip of a used crayon. It is the green eye of God, the one that rests just above her pursed pink lips. It is a pruned planet drowning in galaxy. It is a painted flower pot crumbling under the weight of the growth we put on it. No, no... it is a pea. It's a fucking pea.

Eat it.

PSALM FOR MY BODY

Blessed body,
I kneel before you in deep humility.

This psalm is a tribute and an apology,
a hymn in the key of your rapid heartbeat.

This poem is too little, too late,
but I hope you will let me finish.

Praise be to the shredded cuticles,
a staple on your pamphlet hands.

Grasping therapy worksheets
and stained with indelible, ebony ink.

God bless your Twizzler tongue,
as it can sweeten a man's sour mouth

and satisfy a woman's candied craving.
It's flexible that way.

Blessed body,
I'm terribly sorry.

I've forsaken your birth name,
picked a moniker with more syllables.

I just wanted a beautiful way
to take up space.

Blessed body,
I'll stop talking.

It's your turn.

PARTS OF MYSELF I KILLED TO BE HAPPY

the class clown / the daughter / the sister / the rock / the snake pit in my stomach / the writhing reptiles around my throat / the hard worker / the manic dream / the therapist's nightmare / the split lip / the plyboard belly / the loyal confidant / the love song / the stolen silver / the sucker punch

the parts that once were necessary

the parts I hope I'll never need again

INCOMPLETE LIST OF PLACES
I HAVE SEEN GOD

In the crease of your long lobes, where the base of your ears kiss the crown of your jaw. // At the shabby cinema on Brucke Strasse, bathed in the glow of an old projector and the shadow of a new love. // On the dirt field where the patched ball that gave me a shiner still lies. // Shimmering with the smoke that lingers around my paisley pipe. // Cupped inside my pruned palms at the stream in the Smokies where I swam alone. // Splayed out on the coffee table in a line of high spades. // In the sting of my own sullied knees. // My own mangled cuticles. // My raucous laugh that reverberates in an empty room. //

Have you ever heard something so hollow

and still sworn it was holy?

SAVED

Roach, for the first time,
is not hiding.
Roach doesn't consider herself a pest,
and she doesn't want any man's religion.

She aches to be her own
        higher power,
to cradle all her parts inside her palms.
Let them cuddle together through the day
and   scatter   in the night.

Roach accepts that she's grimy,
a bit b/r/o/k/e/n/.

Roach split herself on purpose,
but it's not a mortal sin to make mistakes.
It's okay to not always know what's best.

Roach learns to appreciate her
off-putting essence
by expanding her concept of family.
She mingles with other strong-willed insects
and her internal engine turns over.

No longer just a sum of her own shards,
but a pinion in a larger vehicle of love —
Roach knows the Higher Self is most efficient
when it works as part of a healthy system.

Roach is meditating at dusk, ready for a night
of roaming, of knowing,
and not knowing   what happens next.

It doesn't matter.

Roach is letting go.

ACKNOWLEDGEMENTS

To the therapists who didn't fear me and the doctors who like difficult cases.

To my friends from recovery — I hope this book finds you in a place of healing, too.

To my Patreon subscribers, who motivate me to keep improving my craft and support me in all my endeavors.

To Seneca Basoalto, for being an honest mentor and teaching me to value my voice.

To Isabelle Correa, for your helpful feedback and continuous inspiration.

Lastly, to Jordyn Krieg and Arcana Poetry Press. You believed in me, and extraordinary things came of it. I cannot express enough gratitude.

ABOUT THE AUTHOR

Prudence Brooks (she/her) is a tender and strange poet born in rural Indiana, now happily nestled among the pines of Portland, Oregon. A queer, disabled woman living with AuDHD, Prudence considers her poetic voice more than a passion — it is a form of unmasking in a world that commands her to assimilate. She is the author of two poetry collections, TRUCE and SAVED, and serves as the grubby-toed host of the Roach Reading Club on Patreon. Her work has appeared in *Pile Press*, *Feral Journal of Poetry and Art*, *Eunoia Review*, *Querencia Press*, *Black Fox Literary Magazine*, *Grey Coven Publishing*, and others. You can find her on Instagram (@prudence.writes) or explore her products and services at prudencewrites.com.

www.ingramcontent.com/pod-product-compliance
Lightning Source LLC
Chambersburg PA
CBHW020420150626
46554CB00014B/2183